TALES FROM BEATRIX POTTER

The Tale of Peter Rabbit, The Tale of Benjamin Bunny,
The Tale of Tom Kitten, and *The Tale of Johnny Town-Mouse*

Teacher Guide

Tessa Tiemann & Tanya Charlton

MEMORIA PRESS

MEMORIA PRESS

www.MemoriaPress.com

TALES FROM BEATRIX POTTER
The Tale of Peter Rabbit, The Tale of Benjamin Bunny,
The Tale of Tom Kitten, and *The Tale of Johnny Town-Mouse*

TEACHER GUIDE
Tessa Tiemann & Tanya Charlton

ISBN 978-1-61538-807-3

First Edition © 2018 Memoria Press | 0319

Cover illustration by Beatrix Potter

CONTENTS

INTRODUCTION

At this stage in reading, students are ready to transition from books with many pictures and fewer words to books with fewer pictures and more text. This *Teacher Guide* provides the tools needed to effectively prepare students to read and to develop vocabulary and comprehension skills. Preparation for reading is critical to success. Simply opening the book and attempting to decode may prove too difficult. However, introduction of phonograms in isolation with the *Phonics Flashcards* and practice with some challenging words pulled directly from the text prior to reading lay the groundwork needed for successful decoding and for developing fluent readers.

TEACHING GUIDELINES: Reading with Phonics

You may adjust this model lesson plan to fit your student(s) and your schedule, whether you teach in a five-day school, a two-day cottage school, or a homeschool. This plan includes Pre-Reading and Post-Reading activities which solidify the phonics lessons and provide additional practice with advanced phonograms students will encounter in the reading. These activities are highly recommended for the classroom; and even for the advanced reader, they are still a good use of time.

Prior to reading the scheduled selection, complete all Pre-Reading activities. After you have read the selection, complete the Post-Reading activities on the following day(s) to give additional practice with the new phonograms and words.

PRE-READING

These activities cover common words, the "Pronounce & Say" and "Vocabulary" words in the *Student Guide*, and any other new or difficult words within the reading.

POST-READING

"Comprehension Questions" can now be completed, and the *Teacher Guide* will include phonics activities that practice select phonograms from the lessons. There will commonly be review of these phonograms in isolation with *Phonics Flashcards* and/or within words from *Classical Phonics*.

NOTES ON READING ACTIVITIES

The transition from phonics and phonetic readers to non-phonetic readers takes careful preparation. These Pre-Reading activities are important to ensure students have the tools they need to be successful. Pre-Reading activities are focused on a) common words and b) new words. Previewing difficult words is the single most effective activity you can do to help your students develop into fluent readers. It is direct and time-efficient. Words that students tend to stumble over should be reviewed as often as necessary.

PRE-READING ACTIVITIES

1. Many of the Common Words in each lesson are found in the Memoria Press *Phonics Flashcards* set, and will be indicated with the flashcard number following the word. For Common Words not found in the *Phonics Flashcards* set, write the word on an index card. Since common words usually have non-phonetic features, they should be drilled as often as needed for your student(s). Students need to know that they can't necessarily sound out every letter in these words and that these words may break rules they have learned. Immediate recall of common words is necessary for reading fluency. (The first page of each lesson in the *Teacher Guide* contains word studies of both common and new words. We have added to the *Teacher Guide* additional new words that are also pulled directly from the text. Use your judgment in deciding how many and which of these new words to emphasize.)

2. New words that might need attention are listed under "Pronounce & Say" in the *Student Guide*. Write these words (or a selection) on the board, making vowels and vowel teams red and consonant teams and blends blue. Go over the pronunciation and meanings. Sound out the regular phonetic features. Recite the words together throughout the week as often as you think necessary.

Syllabication: All multi-syllable words are divided into syllables for you in the *Teacher Guide*. Dividing longer words into syllables helps students to sound out and pronounce unfamiliar words.

Reading: Teachers should do some reading aloud to model good, expressive reading. In the classroom, all students should read aloud. Teachers should make notes of reading fluency and expression for each student and provide additional practice in class or at home if needed.

POST-READING ACTIVITIES

Phonics Flashcards and pages from *Classical Phonics* for some of the new and old phonograms are given here. For instance, in *The Courage of Sarah Noble*, students may not have learned the phonogram **aught**. Now is the opportune time to study this phonogram by looking at the other words with the same spelling pattern. You can write a selection of words on the board and review them all week as students read them together, in pairs, or individually. Or students can read a column of words in *Classical Phonics* together.

Comprehension Questions: Have students read each question and try to formulate a complete answer. If students don't know the answer, help them find it in the text and read it again. Help students develop a good complete answer orally. Write this sentence on the board and have students copy the answer in their guide, using correct spelling and punctuation. Answering questions and composing answers is a valuable learning activity. A question stimulates thinking. Composing an answer requires even more thinking and is a good composition exercise. Speaking well in correct sentences is also a valuable learning activity.

Answers provided in the *Teacher Guide* are thorough. As long as answers are complete and contain appropriate information, use the student's words as much as possible. Do not feel as if students must write everything listed in the *Teacher Guide*. The development of your individual answers is the more important skill.

Model Lesson Plan

PRE-READING:

I. Review

   A. Orally review any previous vocabulary.

   B. Review the plot of the book as read so far to help students remember where they are in the story.

   C. Periodically review the concepts of character, setting, and plot.

II. Study Guide Preview

   A. Pronounce & Say:

- Read aloud together so that students will recognize words when they come across them in their reading. Talk about any words students don't know the meanings of.

   B. Vocabulary:

- Look at each word within the context that it is used, and help your student come up with the best synonym that defines the word. (Make sure it is a synonym the student knows the meaning of.)
- Record the word's meaning in the student's study guide. (Use the student's knowledge of Latin and other vocabulary to decipher meanings.)

READING:

- The student reads the chapter (or selection of the chapter for that lesson) independently or to the teacher (for younger students).
- For younger students, you can alternate between teacher-read and student-read passages. Model good reading skills. Encourage students to read expressively and smoothly. The teacher may occasionally take oral reading grades.
- While reading, mark each vocabulary word as you come across it.
- Have students take note in their study guide margin of pages where a Comprehension Question is answered.

POST-READING:

III. Comprehension Questions

    A. Older students can answer these questions independently, but younger students (2nd-4th) need to answer the questions orally, form a good sentence, and then write it down, using correct punctuation, capitalization, and spelling. (You may want to write the sentence down for the younger student after forming it orally, and then let the student copy it perfectly.)

    B. It is not necessary to write the answer to every question; some may be better answered orally.

    C. Answering questions and composing answers is a valuable learning activity. Questions require students to think; writing a concise answer is a good composition exercise.

IV. Enrichment

    A. The Enrichment activities include composition, copywork, dictation, research, mapping, drawing, poetry work, literary terms, and more.

    B. This section has a variety of activities in it, but the most valuable activity is composition. Your student should complete at least one composition assignment each week. Proof the student's work and have the student copy composition until grammatically perfect. Insist on clear, concise writing. For younger students, start with 2-3 sentences, and do the assignment together. The student can form good sentences orally as you write them down, and then the student copies them.

    C. These activities can be completed as time and interest allow. Do not feel you need to complete all of these activities. Choose the ones that you feel are the best use of your student's time.

The Tale of Peter Rabbit

PRE-READING (pp. 7-35)

Day 1:

☐ New Words: *Flop·sy, Mop·sy, Cot·ton·tail, Pe·ter, Mr. Mc·Greg·or, cur·rant, ga·ther, straight, ra·dish·es, pars·ley, thief, fright·ened*

☐ Syllabication for Pronounce & Say Words: *ac·ci·dent, mis·chief, naugh·ty, cu·cum·ber, dread·ful·ly, a·mongst, un·for·tun·ate·ly*

☐ *Phonics Flashcards:*

soft **c**-*ice*-41
ch-*chick*-51
sh-*ship*-52
th-*thick/thin*-54
nt-*tent*-63
fr-*frog*-75
gr-*grapes*-76
fl-*flag*-81
str-*stripe*-91
ai-*snail*-93
ei-*ceiling*-100
igh-*light*-104
ea-*bread*-110
aught-*taught*-141
ar-*car*-143
or-*north*-149
er-*fern*-155
ed-168 (sailed)
ly-170 (safely)
ə-171
words ending in /ən/-173 (color, paper)

☐ Common Word: *shoes* (*shoe* - #251)

POST-READING (pp. 7-35)

Day 1:

☐ Phonetic Word Study with *Classical Phonics*

   ☐ Compare the words *thief* and *mischief*. Both have the phonogram **ie**. How does the **ie** sound in each word? (long **e** – *thief*; **short i** – *mischief*)

   ☐ *unfortunately, dreadfully* (CP, p. 119 – **ly**)

Pronounce & Say

accident	presently	unfortunately	dreadfully
cucumber	mischief	scuttered	overheard
amongst	young	naughty	camomile

Vocabulary: Write the meaning of each bold word or phrase.

1. She bought a loaf of brown bread and five **currant** buns. _____ berry

2. He went to look for some **parsley**. _____ herb used as food seasoning
_____

3. It was a blue jacket with **brass** buttons, quite new. _____
yellowish metal made of copper and zinc _____

4. Peter **gave himself up for lost**, and **shed** big tears; but his sobs were overheard by some friendly sparrows, who flew to him in great excitement, and **implored** him to **exert** himself.

   a) _____ gave up, lost hope   c) _____ begged, pleaded

   b) _____ cried   d) _____ make an effort

5. Mr. McGregor came up with a **sieve**, which he intended to pop upon the top of Peter.
_____ strainer

6. Also he was very **damp** with sitting in that can. _____ slightly wet

7. The first thing he saw was Mr. McGregor **hoeing** onions. _____ digging or weeding
_____

8. It was the second little jacket and pair of shoes that Peter had lost in a **fortnight**!
_____ period of 2 weeks

9. "One **table-spoonful** to be taken at bedtime." _____
_____ measurement equal to half an ounce or 3 teaspoons

Comprehension Questions: Answer in complete sentences.

1. Why were the little rabbits not allowed to go into Mr. McGregor's garden? _____

   The rabbits knew that their lives were in danger from Mr. McGregor because he caught

   their father and put him into a pie.

2. What did Peter eat while in Mr. McGregor's garden?

   First he ate some _____lettuces_____ and some _____French_____ beans ;

   and then he ate some _____radishes_____ ; and then feeling rather sick, he went to

   look for some _____parsley_____ .

3. Peter felt rather sick because …

   _____ a) … he felt guilty for being very naughty.   __X__ c) … he had eaten so much.

   _____ b) … Mr. McGregor had been chasing him.   _____ d) … he was so hungry.

4. When Mr. McGregor began to chase Peter, Peter rushed all over the garden. Why didn't Peter run out of

   the garden? _____Peter couldn't remember which way to get back to the gate and out of Mr.

   McGregor's garden.

5. In an effort to hide, Peter rushed into the toolshed and jumped into a can. Why was it not a beautiful

   thing to hide in? _____

   The can had water in it, so Peter got wet while he was hiding.

6. Mr. McGregor finally stopped chasing Peter. Why? _____

   Mr. McGregor got tired of chasing Peter, so he went back to work.

7. What did Mr. McGregor do with Peter's little jacket and shoes? _____Mr. McGregor hung Peter's

   clothes up as a scarecrow in his garden to scare the blackbirds away.

PRE-READING (pp. 36-69)
Day 1:

☐ New Words: *spar·rows, ex·cite·ment, im·plored, ex·ert, sieve, in·tend·ed, wrig·gled, per·haps, ker·ty·schoo, i·dea, wan·der, lip·pi·ty, Ben·ja·min Bun·ny, wheel·bar·row, won·dered, fort·night*

☐ Syllabication for Pronounce & Say Words: *o·ver·heard, pre·sent·ly, scut·tered, cam·o·mile*

☐ Common Words: *busy (#203), sure (#255), clothes, sews (sew - #249), friend (#214)*

☐ *Phonics Flashcards:*

y-*candy*-37	**ow**-*bow*-109
soft **c**-*ice*-41	**ch**-*chorus*-120
wh-*whale*-55	**oo**-*moon*-131
sc-*scale*-65	**or**-*north*-149
sp-*spot*-70	**ear**-*earth*-154
pl-*plate*-82	**er**-*fern*-155
ee-*bee*-98	**le**-*apple*-161
igh-*light*-104	**ed**-168 (*petted, sailed*)

POST-READING (pp. 36-69)
Day 1:

☐ Phonetic Word Study with *Classical Phonics*

   ☐ Look at the word *idea*.
   - Is the first vowel long or short? *long*
   - Is the second vowel long or short? *long*
   - Does the last vowel (**a**) make a long sound? *no*
   - What sound does it make? *short **u***

☐ This word is unusual in that **ea** does not make any of the sounds for **ea** that we have learned. What are the most common sounds for **ea**? (long **a** = *steak*; long **e** = *leaf*; short **e** = *bread*)

☐ Compare the **ear** in *tears* and *overheard*. What sound does the **ear** make in each? (*tears* = **ear**, *overheard* = **earth**)

☐ Look at the word *sieve*. The letters **ie** in *sieve* make a short **i** sound. This is the same sound the letters made in the word *mischief*.

☐ Study the word *chamomile*. First look at the word broken into syllables (cham-o-mile). What sound does the **ch** make? (k) Is the first vowel long or short? (short) The next syllable is just a vowel. Is it long or short? (long) The last syllable is the tricky one because the magic **e** should make the vowel **i** say its name. However, it does not. The **i** has the long **e** sound.

☐ *wriggled* (CP, p. 52 – **wr**) and *exert, excitement* (CP, p. 119 – **ex**)

Day 2:

☐ Review as needed.

Language Lesson

- The **Author** is the person who wrote the story.
- The **Illustrator** is the person who drew the pictures in the story.
- The **Setting** of a story is the time and place that the story takes place.
- The **Characters** in a story are the people or animals the story is about.
- The **Plot** of a story is the main story line, the pattern of events.

Fill in the following information about *The Tale of Peter Rabbit*:

1. Author: _____Beatrix Potter_____

2. Illustrator: _____Beatrix Potter_____

3. Setting: _____the rural countryside; no time frame is mentioned and is unnecessary for_

   _the story_____

   _____

4. Major Characters:

   Peter Rabbit

   Mr. McGregor

   _____

   _____

5. Minor Characters:

   Mrs. Rabbit

   Flopsy

   Mopsy

   Cotton-tail

   _____

6. Plot: _____A little boy rabbit has an adventure when he disobeys his mother and sneaks to_

   _Mr. McGregor's farm, where he gets lost and almost caught by Mr. McGregor._____

   _____

   _____

   _____

   _____

Life Lesson

To contrast means to tell how two things are different. Contrast Peter Rabbit's behavior with that of his sisters when their mother left them alone. Who made the best choices? What was the result of Peter's behavior? What was the result of his sisters' behavior?

Mrs. Rabbit told her children not to go to Mr. McGregor's garden, but as soon as she left,

Peter disobeyed her. Flopsy, Mopsy, and Cotton-tail obeyed their mother and spent the

day gathering blackberries. Peter ended up overeating, being chased and almost caught

by Mr. McGregor, losing his clothes, and getting lost. When he got back home, he was ill

and had to take medicine and go to bed. His sisters had a nice evening with a good meal.

Peter should obey his mother the next time.

Activity

Mr. McGregor had a nice garden filled with good things for Peter Rabbit to eat. Draw a picture of the garden you would like to raise. Give your garden a scarecrow dressed in your favorite outfit. Label each row in your garden with the names of the vegetables or fruits growing.

The Tale of Benjamin Bunny

PRE-READING

Day 1 (pp. 7-31):

- [ ] New Words: *re·la·tions, ba·zaar, rab·bit-to·bac·co, lav·en·der, de·scribed, as·sured, tam·o·shan·ter, es·pe·cial·ly, con·trar·y, ha·bit*

- [ ] Syllabication for Pronounce & Say Words: *muf·fe·tees, sug·gest·ed, on·ions, cer·tain·ly, hand·ker·chief, con·se·quence*

- [ ] *Phonics Flashcards:*
  - **y**-*candy*-37
  - soft **c**-*ice*-41
  - soft **g**-*gem*-43
  - **sh**-*ship*-52
  - **tr**-*track*-77
  - **scr**-*screw*-86
  - **ar**-*car*-143
  - **er**-*fern*-155
  - **ci**-*magician*-162
  - **tion**-*addition*-164
  - **ed**-168 (sailed, petted)
  - **ly**-*safely*-170
  - **ə**-171

- [ ] Common Words: *clothes, especially*

- [ ] Discuss the difference between *Mr.* and *Mrs.*

Pronounce & Say

muffetees	handkerchief	suggested	certainly	mortar	opinion
herbs	consequence	onions	vegetables	terrace	ceiling

Vocabulary: Write the meaning of each bold word or phrase.

1. He **pricked** his ears and listened to the trit-trot, trit-trot of a pony.

   pointed them upward; listened attentively

2. A **gig** was coming along the road. horse-drawn, two-wheeled carriage

3. Benjamin Bunny slid down into the road, and set off ... with a hop, skip and a jump ... to call upon his **relations**. relatives; kinfolk

4. Peter's coat and shoes were plainly to be seen upon the scarecrow, topped with an old **tam-o-shanter** of Mr. McGregor's. beret-like cap

5. Benjamin, **on the contrary**, was **perfectly at home**, and ate a lettuce leaf.

   a. different from Peter (opposite in nature) b. comfortable and secure

6. They went along a little walk on **planks**, under a sunny red-brick wall. wooden boards

7. He took a tremendous jump off the top of the wall on to the top of the cat, and **cuffed** it off the basket.

   slapped

8. He observed several things which **perplexed** him. confused; bewildered

9. It looked as though some person had been walking all over the garden in a pair of **clogs**.

   heavy wooden shoes

Comprehension Questions: Answer in complete sentences.

1. Why was Peter dressed in a red cotton handkerchief when Benjamin met him behind the fir-tree?

   Peter's clothes were in Mr. McGregor's garden, being used as a scarecrow. He lost them

   when he was running away from Mr. McGregor.

Day 2 (pp. 32-57):

- [ ] New Words: *a·mongst, lol·ly·pops, pit·ter-pat·ter, pranc·ing, tre·men·dous, neph·ew, ob·served, sev·er·al, per·plexed, ri·dic·u·lous·ly, man·aged, ceil·ing*

- [ ] Syllabication for Pronounce & Say Words: *veg·e·ta·bles, mor·tar, ter·race, o·pin·ion, ceil·ing*

- [ ] *Phonics Flashcards:*

soft **c**-*ice*-41	**ew**-*grew*-135	**ly**-170 (safely)
soft **g**-*gem*-43	**ar**-*car*-143	**ə**-171
pl-*plate*-82	**er**-*fern*-155	**words ending in /ər/**-172 (dollar)
ou-*young*-111	**ed**-168 (sailed)	
ph-*phone*-119	**ing**-169 (sailing, baking)	

2. Why did Benjamin think that Mr. McGregor and his wife had gone out for the day?

Benjamin saw the McGregors leave in a gig and Mrs. McGregor was wearing her best

bonnet, so he assumed they were going off for the day.

3. Upon sneaking into Mr. McGregor's garden, Peter fell from a pear tree. Why did he not get hurt?

Peter fell into a bed of lettuces, so it was quite soft.

4. Why were Benjamin's foot-marks so odd? _____ Benjamin was wearing clogs, so his

footprints would not have looked like a rabbit's.

5. Peter did not seem to be enjoying himself in the garden. Why? Peter was nervous because of his

previous experience in the garden, so he kept hearing noises that could mean danger.

6. Why was Benjamin so at home in the garden? Why didn't Benjamin and Peter climb the pear tree when

leaving the garden? _____ Benjamin was in the habit of coming to the garden with his father,

so he was not nervous about being there. Benjamin said it was not possible to climb the

tree with a load of vegetables.

7. Why was old Mr. Benjamin Bunny carrying a switch? _____ When Benjamin didn't come home

for hours, Mr. Bunny must have expected that Benjamin was misbehaving. He came

prepared to punish Benjamin when he found him.

8. Why was Mr. McGregor perplexed when he returned to the garden? _____ Mr. McGregor was

perplexed because his garden had footprints in it that appeared to have been made by a

tiny pair of clogs. Also, he was confused because the cat had somehow shut herself up

in the greenhouse and locked the door from the outside.

9. When Peter got home, his mother forgave him. Why? _____ Peter's mother was so glad that he

got his clothes back that she forgave him for disobeying her again.

POST-READING

Day 1:

- [ ] Phonetic Word Study with *Classical Phonics*
  - [ ] *onion, opinion* (CP, p. 117 – **i** = **/y/**)
  - [ ] What sound does the letter **i** make in the word *onion*? **/y/**
  - [ ] After reading the word list on p. 117, write words on the board. Have students underline the **i** that makes **/y/**.
  - [ ] *tremendous, ridiculous* (CP, p. 114 – **ou** = /ŭ/)
  - [ ] Look at the word *half*. Which letter is silent? *l*
  - [ ] In the word *nephew*, what two letters make /f/? *ph*
  - [ ] Read some other words in which *ph* makes /f/. (CP, p. 115 – **ph** = /f/)
  - [ ] How is the /f/ written in the word *laugh*? *gh*
  - [ ] Read some other words in which **gh** makes /f/. (CP, p. 115 – **gh** = /f/)

Day 2:

- [ ] Review different ways to write /f/. Give examples of each.
- [ ] List several words from *Classical Phonics*, p. 115 (**ph** = /f/, **gh** = /f/) on the board and play Erase a Word. Students get to erase the words as they read them.

Day 3:

- [ ] Review as needed.

Language Lesson

A sentence has to have a **subject** and a **verb**. The **subject** is the main noun that tells what or who the sentence is about. The **verb** is the word that tells what the subject—the main noun—is doing. The **verb** is an action word.

Peter was sitting by himself.

This sentence is about Peter. Therefore, **Peter** is the subject.

What is Peter doing? Peter is sitting. So **sitting** is the verb.

Underline the <u>subject</u> of each sentence and circle the verb:

1. One morning a little <u>rabbit</u> sat on a bank.

2. <u>He</u> pricked his ears.

3. <u>He</u> listened to the trit-trot, trit-trot of a pony.

4. <u>Little Benjamin</u> sat down beside his cousin.

5. <u>Peter</u> fell down head-first.

6. <u>They</u> winked at Peter Rabbit and little Benjamin Bunny.

Life Lesson

Was Benjamin Bunny's father fair in his punishment of Benjamin? Do you think he enjoyed spanking Benjamin? Why did he feel it was necessary to punish Benjamin for going to Mr. McGregor's farm? Write four good sentences answering these questions in paragraph form. Don't forget to indent.

> Answers will vary. Benjamin's father punished Benjamin because he had placed himself in a dangerous position. The punishment was meant to encourage Benjamin to be more careful in his choices so that he would not put his life in danger. His father loves him and was afraid for him. He could have gotten eaten by the cat or killed by Mr. McGregor. Of course, Benjamin may have learned his lesson by himself since he was so afraid. But his father wanted to make sure he understood the seriousness of the situation.

Activity

Beguiled is a synonym for *tempted*. Benjamin Bunny tempted Peter Rabbit into going to Mr. McGregor's garden. Peter followed Benjamin into Mr. McGregor's garden even though he was nervous and knew he wasn't supposed to be there.

What would you do if someone tempted you to do something you weren't supposed to?

Draw a picture of what you would do below.

Some ideas:

- Your sister tempted you to take a cookie from the cookie jar even though your mom asked you not to eat anything before dinner.

- Your brother told you to hide all your dirty clothes under your bed when your dad asked you to clean up.

- A friend tempted you to make a silly sound when your teacher walked out of the classroom even though she asked you not to make any noise.

The Tale of Tom Kitten

PRE-READING
Day 1 (pp. 7-29):

☐ New Words: *Tab·i·tha Twit·chit, ex·pect·ed, com·pan·y, ar·rived, pin·a·fores, tuck·ers, trous·ers*

☐ Syllabication for Pronounce & Say Words: *naught·y, el·e·gant, un·com·fort·a·ble, un·stead·i·ly, rock·er·y*

☐ *Phonics Flashcards:*

    y-*candy*-37
    ck-*duck*-49
    ch-*chick*-51
    th-*thick/thin*-54
    tw-*twig*-85
    ea-*bread*-110
    ou-*round*-129
    aught-*taught*-141
    ore-*score*-151
    er-*fern*-155
    le-*apple*-161
    ed-168 (sailed, petted)
    ly-170 (safely)
    ə-171

☐ Common Word: *sewed (sew - #249)*

Day 2 (pp. 30-57):

☐ New Words: *Re·bec·cah, Je·mi·ma, ad·vanced, var·i·ous, ar·ti·cles, af·front·ed, dis·turbed, dig·ni·ty, re·pose*

☐ Syllabication for Pronounce & Say Words: *dif·fi·cul·ties, de·scend·ed, mea·sles, con·trar·y, ex·traor·di·nar·y*

☐ *Phonics Flashcards:*

y-*candy*-37	**ou**-*young*-111	**ed**-168
soft **c**-*ice*-41	**ph**-*phone*-119	(*sailed, petted, baked*)
sc-*scissors*-66	**ew**-*grew*-135	**ə**-171
tr-*track*-77	**ar**-*car*-143	**words ending in /ər/-**
pl-*plate*-82	**or**-*north*-149	172 (*dollar*)
ea-*leaf*-99	**ur**-*turkey*-158	

☐ Common Words: *laughed (laugh - #229), friends (friend - #214)*

Pronounce & Say

naughty	sewed	rockery	measles
elegant	pig-stye	difficulties	contrary
uncomfortable	unsteadily	descended	extraordinary

Vocabulary: Write the meaning of each bold word or phrase.

1. But one day their mother … expected friends to **tea**. _____
   an afternoon refreshment of sandwiches and cakes served with tea (chiefly British)

2. Mrs. Tabitha dressed Moppet and Mittens in clean **pinafores** and **tuckers**.

   a) _____ aprons worn by girls as a dress or over-dress

   b) _____ pieces of linen or lace worn around the neck and shoulders

3. Keep away from the dirty **ash-pit** _____ pit where old ashes from fireplaces were thrown

4. He came up the rockery **by degrees** _____ in stages; step by step

5. Mr. Drake Puddle-duck **advanced** in a slow sideways manner. _____ moved forward; progressed

6. "My friends will arrive in a minute, and you are not fit to be seen; I am **affronted**," said Mrs. Tabitha Twitchit.
   insulted; offended

7. Somehow there were very extraordinary noises over-head, which disturbed the **dignity** and **repose** of the tea-party.

   a) _____ decency; respectfulness

   b) _____ calmness; tranquility

Comprehension Questions: Answer in complete sentences.

1. Why did Mrs. Tabitha Twitchit fetch the kittens indoors to wash and dress them?

   Mrs. Twitchit had company coming for tea and wanted her kittens to look nice for

   her friends.

2. List the steps Mrs. Tabitha Twitchit took to wash and groom her kittens.

   First she ___scrubbed their faces___ .

   Then she ___brushed their fur___ .

   Then she ___combed their tails and whiskers___ .

3. Why did Tom Kitten's clothes not fit him?

   _____ a) He was very naughty.   _____ c) He had grown.

   _____ b) He was very fat.   __X__ d) He was very fat, and he had grown.

4. Why did Moppet and Mittens turn their pinafores from back to front?

   Moppet and Mittens were having trouble walking without stepping on their pinafores, so

   they moved them around so that they could move more freely to climb the rockery wall.

5. Mittens laughed so hard she fell off the wall. What made her laugh?

   Rebeccah and Jemima Puddle-duck had put Tom's hat and Moppet's tucker on.

6. The kittens were not fit to be seen by the friends of Mrs. Tabitha Twitchit, so she sent them upstairs. What lie did Mrs. Tabitha Twitchit tell her friends about the kittens' absence?

   Mrs. Twitchit told her friends that the kittens were sick with the measles.

7. "And I think that some day I shall have to make another, larger, book, to tell you more about Tom Kitten!"

   What did the author mean by this? ___Beatrix Potter had more Tom Kitten stories to tell, so___

   she was thinking about writing more stories about Tom for children to read. Tom does

   occur in several more of her books.

POST-READING

Day 1:

☐ Phonetic Word Study with *Classical Phonics*

   ☐ *uncomfortably, unwisely, unsteadily, unable* (CP, p. 119 – **un**)

☐ Write the following words on the board: *contrary, ordinary, dignity, party, very, directly*. Have students read the words, tell how many syllables are in each, and what sound the letter **y** at the end makes.

☐ Compare the sound of the letter **a** at the beginning of the words *advanced, articles,* and *affronted.*

☐ Which of these words begins with ə? *affronted*

☐ Which word begins with the short sound of **a**? *advanced*

☐ What letter changes the sound of **a** in the word *articles*? **r**

Day 2:

☐ Turn to *Classical Phonics*, p. 124. Look at column 1 only. Ask students what is the same about all the words in column 1. *They all begin with an a, which is making the schwa sound.*

   ☐ Have students read that column.

☐ How do the words in column 2 begin? *be*

   ☐ Column 3? *de* Column 4? *o*

Day 3:

☐ Review as needed.

Language Lesson

A **noun** is a person, place, thing, or idea. An **adjective** is a word that describes a noun.

Once upon a time there were <u>three</u> <u>little</u> kittens.

The words that describe *kittens* are **three** and **little**. *Three* and *little* tell us things about the *kittens*, so they are adjectives.

Kittens is a noun.

Underline the <u>adjectives</u> of each sentence and circle the nouns they describe:

1. They had <u>dear</u> <u>little</u> <u>fur</u> coats.

2. Then she took the <u>elegant</u>, <u>uncomfortable</u> clothes out of a chest.

3. She made <u>hot</u> <u>buttered</u> toast.

4. The <u>three</u> Puddle-ducks came along the <u>hard</u>, <u>high</u> road.

5. They had <u>small</u> eyes and looked surprised.

Activity

On a separate sheet of paper, draw a picture of an animal that you own (or an animal that you know) dressed in your clothes. Then make up a story about what your animal did while dressed in your clothes and write it below.

_____

_____

_____

_____

_____

_____

_____

Life Lesson

Several characters in this story have **moral failures**. A **moral failure** is when we do something that conflicts with moral rules. From the list of moral prescriptions below, choose the one that each character disobeyed. Then, write a sentence explaining this disobedience. You will use one prescription twice.

| 1. Do not steal. | 2. Respect your mother and father. | 3. Be honest. |

Tom Kitten: _____

2. Tom scratched his mother while she was bathing him, and he disobeyed his mother by getting dirty and playing with the Puddle-ducks.

Mittens and Moppet: _____

2. Mittens and Moppet also disobeyed their mother by getting dirty and playing with the Puddle-ducks.

Mr. Drake Puddle-duck: _____

1. Mr. Puddle-duck stole Tom Kitten's clothes, put them on, and kept them.

_____

Mrs. Tabitha Twitchit: _____

3. Mrs. Twitchit told a lie to her friends because she was embarrassed that her children looked so bad. She said they were sick when they were not.

In the Activity section of the *Tale of Benjamin Bunny* lesson, you drew what you would do if someone tempted you. Did the person who tempted you break one of the rules above? If not, what rule did he or she break?

_____

_____

_____

_____

The Tale of Johnny Town-Mouse

PRE-READING

Day 1 (pp. 7-33):

☐ New Words: *car·ri·er, six·pence, par·lour, ca·nar·y, in·stant·ly, re·cov·ered, po·lite·ness, in·sig·nif·i·cant, el·e·gant, skir·mish·ing, hor·ror, mis·er·a·ble, rack·et·ted, par·tic·u·lar·ly, pre·vent·ed, thros·tles*

☐ Syllabication for Pronounce & Say Words: *wick·er·work, re·com·mend·ed, anx·ious, ut·most, skirt·ing·board, ex·clu·sive·ly, ap·pe·tite, young·sters, in·tro·duced, in·quired, un·ac·cus·tomed, ex·clam·a·tion, con·tin·u·al, hon·est·ly*

☐ *Phonics Flashcards:*

ī-*kite*-34	**ar**-*car*-143
y-*candy*-37	**ir**-*bird*-156
soft **c**-*ice*-41	**wor**-*worm*-157
ck-*duck*-49	**le**-*apple*-161
sh-*ship*-52	**tion**-*addition*-164
nt-*tent*-63	**ed**-168 (sailed, petted)
sk-*skate*-67	**ing**-169 (sailing)
st-*stamp*-71	**ly**-170 (safely)
thr-*throne*-92	**ə**-171
ea-*bread*-110	**words ending in**
ou-*young*-111	**/ər/**-172 (paper, color)

☐ Common Word: *laughed* (*laugh* - #229)

Day 2 (pp. 34-57):

☐ New Words: *re·fuge, con·ver·sa·tion, en·deav·oured, en·ter·tain, di·ges·tion, un·ac·cus·tomed, huf·fi·ly, with·ered, vi·o·lets, vi·o·lent·ly, mid·dling, par·tic·u·lar, lawn·mow·er*

☐ *Phonics Flashcards:*

y-*candy*-37	**ou**-*young*-111	**ed**-168 (petted, sailed, baked)
soft **c**-*ice*-41	**ph**-*phone*-119	**ə**-171
sc-*scissors*-66	**ew**-*grew*-135	**words ending in /ər/**-172 (dollar)
tr-*track*-77	**ar**-*car*-143	
pl-*plate*-82	**or**-*north*-149	
ea-*leaf*-99	**ur**-*turkey*-158	

Pronounce & Say

wickerwork	anxious	exclusively	introduced	exclamation
recommended	utmost	appetite	inquired	continual
learnt	skirting-board	youngsters	unaccustomed	honesty

Vocabulary: Write the meaning of each bold word or phrase.

1. The gardener sent vegetables to town once a week by carrier; he packed them in a big **hamper**.

   a large basket, usually with a cover

2. The cook gave the carrier **sixpence** ___ a coin worth six pennies

3. the **parlour maid** ran up and down stairs ___ the maid in charge of the parlour (formal room used to entertain visitors - we would call it a living room today)

4. Timmy Willie's own tail was **insignificant**. ___ trivial; small

5. they were too **well bred** to make **personal remarks** a) ___ well-mannered

   b) ___ comments about a specific person

6. two young mice, who were **waiting** on the others, went **skirmishing** upstairs to the kitchen between **courses**.

   a) ___ serving

   b) ___ battling (falling over each other) (skirmish = minor battle)

   c) ___ part of a meal served in units (one at a time)

7. Johnny Town-mouse quite honestly recommended it as the best bed, kept **exclusively** for visitors.

   entirely for the use of; particularly

8. An excellent breakfast was provided … for mice **accustomed** to eat bacon ___ used to, experienced in

9. When they had taken **refuge** in the coal-cellar he resumed the conversation; "I confess I am a little disappointed; we have **endeavoured** to entertain you, Timothy William."

   a) ___ protection, shelter

   b) ___ attempted, tried

Comprehension Questions: Answer in complete sentences.

1. Timmy Willie was a little country mouse who went to town by mistake. How did this happen?

   Timmy Willie took a nap in the basket and didn't wake up until it was being loaded onto a cart.

2. One of the town mice asked Timmy Willie if he had ever been in a trap. Why did he ask this?

Timmy Willie had a short tail, so the mice wanted to know if it was because his tail had

been cut off in a trap. It was a polite way of finding out why Timmy Willie's tail was

short without coming right out and asking him.

3. Why was Timmy Willie so nervous during the eight-course meal? _____ There were many dishes

Timmy Willie had never seen before, so he was nervous about trying them. Also, there

were lots of noises upstairs that Timmy Willie had never heard before. And Timmy

Willie was anxious that he wouldn't behave with proper manners during the meal.

4. How did the town mice get all of the food they ate? _____ The mice got their food from the

kitchen where meals were prepared for the people who lived in the house.

5. If there was so much elegant food to eat, why was Timmy Willie growing so thin while in town?

Timmy Willie was very homesick. The food was unfamiliar and disagreed with his

stomach and the unfamiliar noises made him nervous.

6. Why was Johnny Town-mouse so disappointed? _____ Johnny Town-mouse had done his

best to treat Timmy Willie kindly as his guest, and Timmy Willie responded by growing

thin and sad. This made Johnny Town-mouse feel like he had failed.

7. Johnny Town-mouse inquired about Timmy Willie's garden home and wanted to know what Timmy Willie did when it rained. Why was this question so important for a town mouse?

A town mouse has the shelter of buildings to live in. Since Timmy Willie lived in a

garden, Johnny Town-mouse was concerned about how he got shelter when it rained.

8. What is the main reason Johnny Town-mouse paid a visit to Timmy Willie so early in the season?

The family that lived in Johnny Town-mouse's house was on vacation, and the cook had

been given directions to clear the house of mice while they were gone.

9. Why didn't Johnny Town-mouse want to live in the country? _____

Johnny Town-mouse said the country was too quiet.

POST-READING
Day 1:

☐ Phonetic Word Study with *Classical Phonics*

  ☐ Write the following words on the board in one column: *inquired, instantly, insignificant, instructions.* (CP, p. 119 – **in**)

  ☐ Write the following words on the board in an adjacent column: *endeavored, entertain.*

  ☐ Read each column. Compare the spelling of the initial syllable. They sound the same but are spelled differently. Can you think of other words which belong in either column?

  ☐ Look at the word *parlour*. In Beatrix Potter's day, the parlour was a special room of the house that was kept clean and tidy. It was the place visitors sat to have tea and talk. Over time the spelling has changed to *parlor*, and means a private room for relaxation.

Day 2:

☐ This book had several multi-syllabic words. Write the words from the New Words or Literature Guide words on index cards. Divide the class into teams. When a student correctly reads their card, they get a point for their team.

Day 3:

☐ Review as needed.

Language Lesson

1. The city was too loud for Timmy Willie. Find and circle the action words below that tell about the noises of the city.

> … the back door banged, and the cart rumbled away. But there was no quiet …
>
> Dogs barked; boys whistled in the street; the cook laughed, the parlour maid ran up
>
> and down stairs; and a canary sang like a steam engine.

2. What kinds of words are action words? _____

   Verbs
   _____

3. Next, find the words that tell who or what was making the noises and underline them.

> … the back door banged, and the cart rumbled away. But there was no quiet …
>
> Dogs barked; boys whistled in the street; the cook laughed, the parlour maid ran up
>
> and down stairs; and a canary sang like a steam engine.

4. What kinds of words tell who or what is doing the action? _____

   Nouns
   _____

5. The city is louder than the country, but the country has its own set of noises. When Johnny Town-mouse visits the country, he hears noises that frighten him. Use action words to complete the sentences about the noises Johnny Town-mouse hears in the country.

   A cow _____, and Johnny Town-mouse was frightened. Then a

   lawnmower _____, and Johnny Town-mouse was startled again.

Life Lesson

Politeness to guests is called "hospitality." When Timmy Willie "dropped in" on the city mice, they treated him with great hospitality. And Timmy Willie returned the favor by treating Johnny Town-mouse with respect and kindness.

Name some of the ways Johnny Town-mouse and Timmy Willie showed politeness and good manners toward each other.

Johnny Town-mouse politely introduced Timmy Willie to the guests at the dinner party.

The guests politely refrained from commenting on Timmy Willie's shorter tail. Timmy

Willie ate food at the dinner that he wasn't sure he would like. The best bed in the house

was given to guests, so Timmy Willie had the honor of that bed. When Timmy Willie

was homesick, Johnny Town-mouse felt like he had failed as a host, but Timmy Willie

assured Johnny Town-mouse that he had been most kind to him.

_____

_____

Have you ever had guests stay at your house? Write one or two sentences telling how you made them feel at home by showing hospitality.

_____

_____

_____

_____

_____

_____

Activity

Johnny Town-mouse did not want to live in the country, and Timmy Willie was not happy in the city. Make a list of the differences between the country and the city.

City	Country
_____	_____
_____	_____
_____	_____
_____	_____
_____	_____
_____	_____

Which do you prefer, the city or the country? Explain.

_____

_____

_____

_____

_____

_____

_____

Draw a picture of your favorite place to live.

Where did you choose? _____